Finding Your Fortune

Bridging the gap between you
and your financial freedom

by Sparkle Phillips

Proudly Published in the USA by
Thornton Publishing, Inc
17011 Lincoln Ave. #408
Parker, CO 80134

Phone: (303)-794-8888
Fax: (720)-863-2013

www.ForTheWealthOfAll.com
publisher@bookstobelievein.com

Dedication

To you –
may this help
you truly find
your fortune!

Keep a Journal

As you read this and I share my insights with you, I know that you will be relating some of your memories to mine. If you catch yourself doing that, write these memories down in the journal at the back of the book. Please don't judge these memories, just write them down.

As the book progresses, you may find deep significance in these memories (and you may not). As memories spark in you, trust that there is a reason and it will become clear eventually.

Relax and go with the flow of your thoughts.

Table of Contents

Introduction

The missing piece in the popular manifesting programs

Most people don't *really* believe there's a way to get there.

I listened to abundance teacher after abundance teacher from Wallace Waddles to T. Harv Eker, and learned great things from each and every one of them, but no matter how many times I listened to those talks, I still didn't think I was rich and I knew I wasn't financially free.

"You're as rich as you choose to feel right now," was a saying that I heard over and over and over again.

And I resented that statement usually grumbling something like, "Great, it's all on me again. It's about *my attitude*. It's about how I 'label myself'." I could go around all day and exclaim, "I'm rich, I'm prosperous!" but when my bills found me and I had to dole out almost everything I had to pay them, I didn't feel very rich and financial freedom was a complete pipe dream.

I needed something more than "attitude coaching". I needed real answers to real financial issues. I didn't understand why these financial gurus just couldn't teach me what I needed to know to go to the next level without me having to make the first big seemingly impossible mental step. Why couldn't *they just give* me something to help me up there instead of telling me it is all in my thoughts and in my mind?

For me, the problem was that while I was living paycheck-to-paycheck, "financial freedom" wasn't the next level up – being able to sleep peacefully at night was. In fact, financial freedom was closer to four or five 'levels' away. Still, all of these abundance teachers believed that anyone could make it to that sublime level of complete financial freedom. And absolutely, I do agree, they're right. However, *I* needed to see the path, not just the destination.

"You'll see it when you believe it," was their mantra.

"I'm trying to believe. I'm trying to believe!" was my frustration. The worst part was, I knew they were absolutely right, but they still weren't giving me the one necessary piece I needed to get there – the HOW!

"It's up to the Universe, don't worry about the 'how'," was the response from the book-de-jour. "The Universe will handle it, you just have to visualize the money coming to you and the 'how' doesn't matter." That sounded like a fairy tale or more like Santa Claus.

I knew I had to believe before I could manifest the money into my life, but I still didn't have what I truly needed – something/anything solid to hold on to. I couldn't see any realistic way that my situation could change.

Living in that reality was what kept me down for so long – until I decided I was the one who had to create my own possible set of 'hows'.

Those brilliant authors are still all perfectly correct,

but until I had a 'how' that I could hold on to, I couldn't get to that one necessary, believable vision that would lift me up out of my circumstances into a better financial future.

I'm willing to bet that most people are just like me. When they are looking for a way to make more money or are going through abundance training, they are in a position to *need more money*. They are obviously in a position of lack and wanting more abundance to flow into their experience. Someone telling them to 'just believe' frankly sounds like a recipe for disaster. They're already surrounded by dream stealers who are destroying their self-confidence, the self-confidence they'll truly need if they are going to be able to pull themselves out of their current situation. Paying money to have some one tell them to sit around 'trying to find a happy place' will probably cause the volume on those dream stealers to be deafening – especially those voices already inside their own heads. I speak from experience...

So, how do you bridge the gap?

This is what needs to happen.

You *do* need to believe.

You need to believe in something believable.

How do you bridge the gap from your current circumstances to a believable prosperous position? How do you get from a place of lack to a place where truly believing that abundance is possible is an easy path to follow?

You have to live in your day-to-day circumstances. These prosperity teachers teach that you can not put your attention on your day-to-day circumstances if you want to get to a better place. Yet, if you see no hope – no 'how' – to get from here to there, the exercise is, quite frankly, pretty futile.

What I decided I must do was to find something I could really believe in and let that take me to the place of believing. I had to increase the believability factor of my personal abundance. I had to find a 'how' that I could believe in... because the hope that was generated from that *could* get me to a place of peace, a place of being able to visualize and to a place where I could quiet my own private dream-stealers. It didn't matter if that vision ever came true or panned out. What did matter was if I could imagine that I had an actual vehicle that could take me from here to there.

This book is intended to create just such a vehicle for you.

Chapter 1

You do have to change

If you really wanted it...

If you read my other book – "Finding Your Soul Mate," you'll remember the part of the book where the teacher had us imagine what we really, really wanted and then let us know the real truth about it.

"If you *really* wanted it, you'd have it by now."

There is some payoff for you for not having what you say you want – identify what it is and decide if that payoff is more important to you than your desire. Or examine the possibility that the payoff for not having it isn't really as mutually exclusive to your goal as you thought.

It's easy to understand... There is a disconnect between what you say you want and what you truly want. It is because something else is more important.

Usually the 'something more important' is you. There is some type of fear driving your psyche 'to protect you from all the problems that money can bring'.

Ask yourself, "If I had an incredible amount of money in the bank, would I be afraid...

❖ ...of someone else's opinion of me?" *The "What will the neighbor's think?" syndrome?*

❖ ...of losing it and having nothing to show for it?" *Maybe you'll spend it on something frivolous, then you'll hear all those old criticisms of you again.*

❖ ...of someone taking it?" *If you get rich, will the distant family come out of the woodwork and suddenly need your money? Will that just create more hassles than you're willing to deal with?*

❖ ...of being ignorant about handling money?" *If you've never had a great deal of money, you're going to have to start learning about lots of new things – banks, types of accounts, lots of financial jargon. Does that aspect of being rich feel overwhelming?*

❖ ...of becoming a target if you have money?" *Do you believe criminals target the wealthy? (No – they target opportunity. The wealthy build in safe-guards to protect what they own.)*

You need to do a serious self-inventory and decide if fear or something else is holding you back. If it is fear, like anything else, really examine those fears and determine a course of action. Once you know what you'd do 'if' any particular fear was to manifest – typically, those fears lose their power.

Figure out what your payoff is for not having an abundance of money in your life. Do the following exercise and see if you glean any insight.

Imagine you just watched the winning lotto numbers roll across the TV screen and you just realized you won all the money. Stop for a moment. Take a deep breath. Revel right there. Stay in the moment. Read this paragraph again and pause right here – stay in this moment.

You just won millions of dollars.

You just won millions of dollars!

YOU JUST WON MILLIONS OF DOLLARS!!!

Everything just changed for you.

Take another deep breath. Okay, one more breath for good measure – let it sink in. You just won millions of dollars!!!

Now make a decision or two.

Who is the first person you call? Your mother, your lawyer, your best friend? Are you going to tell anyone? **You don't have to.**

At this moment in time, you are completely in control of who knows and who doesn't know. So, if you're worried about how someone might react – you don't have to tell them. Your finances are a very private matter. If you have problem people in your life – don't tell them. Do you think they'd tell you if they won a ton of money? You don't owe anyone an explanation. You control your own destiny.

So, now, who is your first phone call to?

Did the answer change?

Did any of those fears go away?

Your prosperity is your business!

Just for the record...

My biggest excuse was that my parents had instilled a deep fear in me. They'd instilled the fear of having money because it would make me a target of the 'bad people.' There were plenty of examples of it in the news – robbery, the occasional kidnapping and any celebrity that was ever murdered. Even if I didn't know the real story behind these news stories, I could always rationalize that it was about money and go back to my sour-grapes response, "Glad I don't have that problem."

Then one day, I came to the realization that it is much safer to be rich than to be poor. As a poor person, I was still a target. I was a target for the bill collectors, loan sharks, credit card companies, insurance companies and banks. They could take advantage of me because I didn't have the resources to pay them off. I came to the realization that it is much safer to be rich because I could protect myself from the likes of them. Plus, I could afford a security system if I truly wanted it and I could hire the right people to keep my finances confidential.

> **"We can't solve problems with the same kind of thinking that we used when we created them."** ~Albert Einstein

Using that logic, you can't create prosperity using the same mind-set as the one that got you in the paycheck-to-paycheck rut. You can't learn how to be abundant from people who are not already abundant. If your parents or your friends aren't where you want to be financially – stop listening to their advice. If your parents or friends are financially free – then, by all means, listen and learn well.

"Take my advice – I'm not using it..."

There are always tons of people willing to give out free financial advice. I finally learned to ask the question, "How's that idea working for you?"

The answer usually is, "It isn't working for me. I'm just trying to help."

As my husband always says, "They mean well..."

Again, if they're mega-rich, you might want to listen, however...

Do you want your situation to change?

If you think you're doing everything right, and the

world is against you and you're not willing to change to get out of this mess, then please, just go return this book right now. Whoever you bought it from will give you a complete refund.

If you think the problem is outside of you, you will not be able to move forward. Until you come to terms with that perspective, your situation won't change.

Let's talk about the next step.

Okay, you're still here. I'm glad.

Have you ever blamed anyone else for your predicament?

If you've ever blamed someone or something outside of yourself for your situation, I want to show you that the external world isn't to blame.

Who/what are the culprits you might have come to believe are the reasons that you can't make more money? Maybe you've been told something all of your life. Maybe the only person saying them to you is you. Maybe you're surrounded by dream-stealers who like the status-quo, and you getting rich would upset their apple cart. So, now, whether you're taking responsibility or blaming others, just brainstorm... what do you believe about who is responsible for your present financial situation?

❖ The government?

❖ The economy?

❖ Your parents?

❖ Your lack of schooling?

❖ Your girlfriend/boyfriend/wife/husband is high maintenance?

❖ Your boss?

❖ Your town?

❖ Your kids' needs come first?

❖ Your medical history?

❖ You've failed before?

❖ You don't want to pay more taxes?

❖ **The government? The economy?** No, plenty of opportunities exist, plenty of people are getting rich even in this economy. Problems need solutions and many people get rich when a problem exists because they decide to solve it instead of complain about it.

❖ **Your parents?** No, plenty of people living paycheck-to-paycheck have a sibling or two who are better off financially than they are. They had the same parents.

❖ **Your lack of schooling?** No, plenty of great wealth was made from people who had very little schooling. JR Simplot, who dropped out of school at age 14 died a billionaire. JR Simplot – the guy who got rich from selling potatoes to Ray Kroc – said this, "You don't have to be smart, just surround yourself with people who are smarter than you are." Go to Idaho someday and look at all the buildings, parks and stadiums that were named after this dropout, turned billionaire, turned philanthropist.

❖ **Your partner is high maintenance?** No, one good manifestor in the family, is enough. They can not 'un-manifest' what you bring into your experience. If you really want to impress them, then make this leap of faith. Make more money than they're used to spending! That's a fun thought – eh?

❖ **Your boss?** No, your job is not your only source of income. If you're living paycheck-to-paycheck, it might feel like that, but there are so many other ways to make money, your boss can't hold you back from your destiny.

❖ **Your town?** No, even if you grew up in a small town, and see no way out of it, money doesn't flow through your town to get to you. It may feel like the energy of the town is oppressive, and if that is the case, then keep your abundance work to yourself and don't look to the townsfolk for understanding or approval. You might not receive it if you sought it and you don't need anyone else's understanding or approval to make this work for you. Once you've reached your goals, show up at a town meeting and when they need a sponsor for an event, stand up – you'll receive approval then... However, it might be smarter to do an anonymous donation if in any way you are hanging on to the fear of distant relatives or needy friends coming out of the woodwork...

❖ **Your kids?** No, but I will grant you that children's needs are immediate. However, if you have children in your life that you want to provide for, learning the way this works and then teaching them how this works is the best motivation I can think of. But just like on airplanes in a crisis, put your own oxygen mask on first, then assist your children. Don't share these ideas with your children until they've worked for you first – they'll need your leadership and when they're ready to create abundance for themselves, they'll seek you out. You can't make abundance for someone else from your own place of lack.

❖ **Your medical history?** No, there are many very inspiring examples of people who suffer medical hardship and live to tell about it, and also live to sell their story in some fashion – maybe in a book or a movie, who knows, but things do happen for a 'good reason' and once you can embrace that truth and be grateful, opportunities will arise out of what others might call disaster. Read "Spiritual Engineering" by Thomas Strawser and see if you agree.

❖ **You've failed before?** No, because whatever you've tried before served to teach you something and you're better for the lesson. Learn to be grateful for the lessons and press on. The great Thomas Edison was quoted as saying, "I never failed at inventing the lightbulb, but I did find 10,000 ways not to." If there is a naggy little voice is inside your head or inside your house, you'll need to find a way to quiet it. After you understand these principles, you'll have better tools to work with. You can learn to replace the naggy little voices with positive words of encouragement – you're your inner-millionaire. You're not the same person you were when you experienced that past lesson, so let the voices of the past fade and let better voices be heard.

❖ **You don't want to pay more in taxes?** No, think this one through. If you have more income, yes, likely your tax bill will also increase, but it will increase in proportion to what you're bringing home. Plus if you start doing many of the things listed in this book, then you'll have tax deductions you never had before, enabling you to keep a greater percentage of your increased income. Then, consider this – you'll probably be able to afford an accountant who will save you more in taxes than the fee you pay them to figure it out. Start thinking like a rich person and forever release this sour-grapes excuse.

Silence the dream stealers in your life

Most people will classify "dream stealers" as those people who constantly belittle you or tell you that your dream is no good. If you have those types of people in your life, you do need to find a way to neutralize their affect on you. However, the biggest dream stealers in your life are those excuses you have been holding on to.

In my book, *"Finding Your Soul Mate,"* I created a little ceremony for all the men in my life and found a way to be grateful for them for all the things they taught me. So, I wrote each of their names on a piece of paper, along with the lesson I learned – such as 'I deserved to be treated better' – and then I lit the BBQ. I burned each one of the pieces of paper, one by one. I let that person go out of my life, with no regrets for his having been a part of my life. He'd been there for a reason, to teach me something useful.

As far as finances go, the excuses were like the old boyfriends. Until I learned the lesson that each one wanted to teach me and could be grateful for the lesson, I couldn't move on to bigger and better.

I did the worst thing anyone can do when manifesting money into my life... I kept score. I'd try something for a day, and if I didn't see a demonstration of insta-money in my life, one of these old excuses would gladly step up to the plate and take a swing at my ideals.

So, I stopped scoring, I released the excuses with gratitude and I moved on to the next step. Whether you go through a formal ceremony or just soul search and journal your new awarenesses, please take the time to figure out the main excuse you've been holding on to, what it truly means and then be grateful for the lesson.

Get in touch with
your inner-millionaire

The concept of having an inner child is well documented through the psychological journals and has been for decades. The concept of having an inner critic is also widely accepted. Now, I give you the concept of your 'inner millionaire'!

All of our inner children just want to come out to play and make life fun to live again. Our inner millionaire is the one prodding you to learn these lessons so that it can be released and live the life it knows you want to lead. Your inner millionaire wants you to learn and live these lessons and is willing to help you get there. Start listening to your inner millionaire – and let it buy your inner critic a permanent vacation to some far away place!

Remember -
Money isn't brains

Far too often, people who have a little bit more money than those around them are looked up to for more than just having accumulated money or created wealth. Many times, this is mistaken for intelligence. It isn't. People with money need to be blessed and you need to learn what you can from their personal experience, but if they are handing out advice about money beyond their personal expertise, it is wise to get a second opinion.

Many of the dream stealers in your life are people with a little bit more money than you have. They like it that way – being richer than you. Their status quo is that they are looked up to more, and given credit for being very smart. As soon as someone else has more money, even if it is merely the potential for more money, it will make them uncomfortable – possibly unconsciously. It may turn them into a more active dream stealer. Just be sure that you give them the respect they are due and bless them for what they have. If they return the blessing, that is terrific, however, don't count on it. Don't change your behavior if indeed they don't share your perspective.

I don't want to be rich – rich people are crazy!

It's true, not all rich people behave well. The news typically reports bad news. So, we tend to hear about the small percentage of rich people who have problems rather than the vast majority of rich people who are happy and stable. There is always a glut of news stories about rock stars or movie stars who destroy hotel rooms or who get into drugs or live a frivolous – what most would consider – wasteful life. There is also a tendency for the media and the movies to portray rich people as powerful and ruthless. I don't want to be like that – and probably you don't either.

So, the answer to this quandary is to find and re-associate the word 'rich' with people you can respect like the philanthropic, admirable, good-hearted people.

Think about the last disaster the country experienced. Did some celebrity step forward and give a generous donation to help? Did a group of entrepreneurs volunteer their time to assist those affected? Did someone of means set up a foundation to support an ongoing relief effort? Yes, Yes, Yes, Yes. Almost every time there is something to be accomplished and money is needed, some person of means steps forward to help out. They make the news too, but not nearly as often, because unlike the people who crave the negative attention, the generous ones didn't do it to receive recognition – they did it because they have really good hearts and the easiest and most effective way they could help was to help financially. So they did. The vast majority of people with means are like this, silent, humble and generous.

Look at the philanthropic people – Oprah, Bill Gates, Warren Buffet, Sandra Bullock – they don't make news as often, but they are known for doing great things.

What if I lost it?

What if you lost it? How many millionaires' and billionaires' stories include a chapter about winning big and losing even bigger and then winning even bigger after that? The beauty of getting rich once, is that you learn the lessons you need to be able to do it again and again. The gift in losing it, if that happens, are lessons that you won't repeat a second time – as long as you truly learn the lessons.

TV isn't helping you get rich

In fact, it is just the opposite. TV is full of sitcoms and drama where people are making fun of each other, hurting or killing each other and these shows generally glorify the cause of struggling through life.

Not all, but many prosperity programs' first main step to the path of prosperity is to turn off the TV and spend that same amount of time working for yourself. True, everyone needs to relax, but there are many other ways to relax that don't involve sitting in front of a television set and letting your mind get numbed.

Think about that crime drama that you really love. How did you feel right after you finished watching it? Uplifted or uneasy? Were you left wondering if that kind of crime could happen to you or someone you love? Did you go to bed wondering about it, or worse, dreaming about it?

What about the last sitcom you watched? You laughed at some of the jokes, but probably because the jokes hit a little too close to home and they made you uncomfortable and laughing releases nervous tension. If it hit really close to home, did it remind you of some problem you have? Even after you turned it off, instead of feeling refreshed and entertained, did you feel even more uneasy about your situation?

Neither one of those types of television shows leaves you in a positive space. You need to be where you're considering your potential and encouraged about your prospects. To truly manifest riches in your life, you need to feel good about your prospects and positively contemplate your potential as much as you possibly can.

Stop watching the news. Don't sit there and be fed fear and resentment. The news is slanted to create resentments, and remind you of your inadequacies – so that 'they' can sell you 'their' products. The news is slanted, either to the far right or the far left depending on your perspective and the channels that you watch. It is full of stories that don't apply to your situation as the news must appeal to a broad viewer base. There is a better place to get the news that you care about, and that is the Internet. Targeted news feeds for your town, your profession, your interests and personal preferences are easy to set up and to use as your source of information. Another great benefit of this way of obtaining your news is that you get to do it on your own time schedule and only spend as much time as you want to. It is just one more way you can start to feel like you're controlling your own destiny and claiming more and more personal time and power over your own life.

Many people will argue that sitting watching TV helps them relax. Maybe that's true to some extent. You do need to know how to relax, clear your mind and refresh. It is important to your overall health and success. So, here's one better suggestion to help you unwind. Take a walk.

Maybe it is because we believe it is going to happen, but almost every time my husband and I go out for a walk, we find money on the ground. Finding those pennies, nickels, dimes and quarters helps remind us that when we're in the proper mind-set, we're truly money magnets.

Stop entertaining your friends with your problems.

Keep your fears to yourself,
but share your courage with others.
- Robert Louis Stevenson

Did you ever ask someone, "How are you?" and even while those words were still being uttered, you wished you could pull them back in? Because you knew that person was going to actually tell you 'how they were' – meaning they were about to do a laundry list of all their current problems and expect you to listen, because you asked for it!!! How does it feel right after a download like that? Did you really need to know those things about that person? Do they just like to complain? We all need to be more aware of how much crap we actually try to unload on other people. In an effort to have less of this deluge of other's problems put on you, start creating boundaries regarding what you put on them. You'll find your conversations and moods start to shift in a better feeling, more positive direction.

The biggest proponents of the Law of Attraction will tell you that "You get what you think about all day long." So, if all you can talk about is how someone at work is treating you poorly, or how your boss or boyfriend doesn't appreciate you, then that is what you are going to get more of.

On the other hand, good begets good, talking about good things begets others talking about good things, which creates uplifted feelings which creates uplifted circumstances. So, instead of asking someone, "How are you?" and expecting them to tell you all their woes, switch it up on them and ask, "What's the good news?" and watch their answers, their mood and your corresponding mood change for the better. If they go down the wrong road and start complaining, put your filter up and say, "I asked for good news!" Either they comply or you leave the conversation. They'll learn, but you need to mean it when you say it.

On the other hand, working to evoke sympathy or empathy from someone else, because you're down, further entrenches your problem into your psyche. When you share it with other people, the problem not only ingrains it deeper into your circumstances, but like a contagion, it also pollutes other people's thoughts, moods and circumstances. Stop using the bad or frustrating parts of your life as punch lines at parties. Stop letting others do it to you.

Not everyone will understand you working to change the focus of your conversation, however, you'll see it is pretty easy to control once you become aware of the feel of a negative conversation. Suddenly, it will feel very uncomfortable to stay in those surroundings and if you can't redirect them, you'll find ways of tuning it out, or you'll find yourself physically leaving the area. Pretty quickly, you'll see a major, permanent, positive shift in your thoughts.

Change your terminology

Certain words carry with them baggage from your past. If you talk to someone about Money vs. Capital, you realize that you are having two completely different feeling conversations. "Needing money for a business venture" or "Raising capital for business venture" both essentially mean the same thing, however, one is typically better received and feels a lot more business-like than the other. I'll let you figure out which one I mean…

Most rich people would consider themselves affluent or prosperous. But the terms affluent and prosperous don't carry the same, typically negative connotations that the word 'rich' does when you're talking about a lifestyle or a person. Affluent or prosperous – at least to me – sounds more elegant, more responsible and more reliable. Compare the phrases 'get rich quick' to 'prosperity programs.' When you start putting labels on the 'you' you want to become, go for the labels that don't carry baggage with them.

Guilt – it's hard to manifest when you're feeling guilty

In many of the prosperity programs, they spend a great deal of time helping you remember your personal greatness, your worthiness. But if you have guilt from a past situation, it is hard to feel worthy.

If someone asked you, "Are you worthy to receive great riches?" What would your internal voice say, "A worthy person wouldn't be in this much debt." Or "A worthy person wouldn't have been divorced twice." Or "A worthy person would still be on speaking terms with her sister." Etc... how does that little dream-stealing voice inside your head guilt you?

If you know you owe someone money that you haven't paid back, or you know that you have a lingering problem with someone else, and it weighs on you, you must find a way to eliminate these feelings from your psyche.

Create a plan to pay the person back after you've made 'x-amount' of money... no old debt gets your first monies – you get that! You start to pay off old debt, after you've shored up your everyday living. But you do make a plan to pay it off. Once you've made the plan – put it out of your head. You'll remember it when the time comes.

However, if you can, start paying a debt back, even if it is in small installments, you'll find you feel freer doing this than ignoring or dodging any old debt. If the person you owe won't take small payments – then just cling to the plan you create.

If you have a lingering personality problem with someone else and that is keeping you from your feeling of worthiness, you need to find a way to extract them from your conscious thoughts. If you can't eliminate them from your thoughts because they are too much a part of your life, then build a 'psychological fence' around them and only allow them in your thoughts at very specific times – say from 10-10:15 AM. If they cross your mind during other times of the day, put them back inside their 'fence'. It is a way of creating a mental boundary around something that is bothering you and compartmentalizing it so that during the rest of the day, you free yourself to think of the things that will help you build your bridge to financial freedom.

You don't always have to answer your phone.

Remember, you are paying for your phone for *your* convenience. No one has the right to intrude on your life through your phone to make you feel bad. When bill collectors or relatives, or other troubling people in your life call you, and you know their purpose is to serve their own agenda, don't answer the phone. If fulfilling their agenda doesn't fit what you are doing at the moment, or if it would be detrimental to something positive you are working on, let the phone call go. Call them back at your convenience. Take control of your life, your thoughts and your communications. It will help you stay on the positive track.

From this moment on, do your best to keep your obligations, clear up the crap from the past and concentrate on the fact that you are more than worthy enough to receive great things in your life. Start to expect more great things from your life and amazingly enough, the Universe will deliver.

Watch what songs
you listen to.

I have a warning in my book *"Finding Your Soul Mate"* about choosing the songs you sing along to with all your heart and soul very carefully. It is the same here. There are many songs that just don't help the cause of getting rich – some that people identify with far too often. My first husband loved the song, "I've got friends in low places." Cute song, sang it many times with him, but if you listen to the lyrics – it is not a song that helps manifest riches. "9-5," "Take this job and shove it," and "Bad Day" and so many more just bemoan circumstances and dwell on the negative side. "I Want to be a Billionaire" has visualization of great things (at least for the singer) in the lyrics. It is a much more positive manifesting song. Any song about gratitude will help you get to a more positive place. In general, just be aware of the vibration of any song you listen to. If it is depressing or angry, it isn't helpful. It is upbeat, it is more helpful for you to change your circumstances for the better. Creating an awareness of all the things in your environment that either help build you up or tear you down is one of the first pieces of knowledge that will help you create the environment you need to create to manifest great things in your life.

Chapter 2

Sources of Inspiration

Huna Philosophy:
"Bless that which you want"

Look at abundant people differently – instead of being jealous, resentful or lustful – see them as sources of inspiration.

When I was reading the Secrets of the Millionaire Mind by T. Harv Eker, he referenced the Huna Philosophy. Huna is the Hawaiian word for 'secret'. There are several rules, principles that determine this philosophy, but one main is, **"Bless that which you want."**

I don't tend to notice luxury cars, because I'm not a car fanatic. However, if someone cuts me off in traffic and they're driving a luxury car, I used to accuse them of 'Thinking they owned the road.'

I didn't accuse lesser cars of that sin. I just complained of my perception of their lack of driving skills.

Why did the 'rich' people deserve such extra ire? They didn't. I had been accustomed to assigning a sense of entitlement to people who had more than I did because they had the audacity to flaunt it by buying rich and fancy cars.

Did I ever see myself driving one of those? No – what waste! I could buy 3 normal cars for the price of their one. I was keeping the experience of owning a luxury vehicle away from me, by complaining about the others who already owned them.

When I learned about the Huna philosophy, I was grateful because something actually articulated my problem. I needed to bless what I wanted instead of curse others that already had it.

I had to bless everyone who already had abundance – whether I perceived they used it appropriately or not.

I had to bless everyone who already had abundance whether I agreed with their politics or not.

I had to bless everyone who had abundance regardless of the way the abundance came to them.

I had to bless everyone who had achieved the level of abundance I desired.

If I didn't, I pushed it away. Once I understood the Huna Philosophy, I could feel when I was attracting or repelling abundance when I encountered it in others. It gave me an awareness I had previously lacked and allowed me to make a conscious shift.

I was able to be grateful for what I had, but I could also be grateful for what every one else had too. It was such a profound shift in my thinking. It was a critical piece to my achieving abundance.

Bless you in your quest for knowledge about abundance and prosperity – as I believe that I will always be searching for new ways to make more money and to enjoy sharing the tools I discover which will help me teach others to do the same.

For your first exercise in the Huna philosophy – bless

every author that you've read or every inspirational speaker you've listened to and bless them in their prosperity and be grateful for their desire to share their life lessons with you – so that your abundance can come to you easily and effectively.

Firewalk story

After I heard about the Huna Philosophy, I started to reconnect with some childhood memories of mine about Polynesia and the way that the Islanders looked at the world. I remembered the movie "South Pacific." I remembered a specific set of scenes in South Pacific that dealt with the idea of the Firewalk. The legend was, if you could walk across fire without getting burned, then you were 'pure of heart', but if you could not, the burns would never heal and your life was cursed.

I was a good manifestor – within one day of learning the Huna Philosophy and connecting with those memories, I found a chance to do a Firewalk at the Community Education center in my city. I had to do it. I had to test myself, so I went.

The teacher walked on broken glass and talked for quite some time to prepare us for what we would face walking across the hot coals. It was a fun lecture with a few very memorable moments, like when he jumped off a chair onto the glass shards and didn't get cut. He did tell us his secret and yes, there is one – don't try this at home!!!

There are many steps in the Firewalk as you traverse the coals, but there are two steps that are the most important – the first, and of course, the last. The first, making the commitment and going for it. That first step is huge. The last step is important as well because it shows you that you have completed it, you carried through, you kept your commitment to yourself.

Once we had done the Firewalk, I was amazed. I had walked across live coals and I had not been burned. It was a validating moment for me.

There was one more statement of the instructor's that has stuck with me since that night and that was his observation of rich people throughout history. "Rich people have good posture, you never see a rich person slumping over when they walk or sit or speak. So when I'm in manifesting mode, I make sure I always sit up straight."

Remember that statement, I'll address that more in a bit... if you want to sit up straight, that's okay too.

However, take a moment and think - Is there something that you've noticed about rich or affluent people that you can emulate and therefore more closely identify with them?

* Do most, or all of them, dress nice?

* Do most, or all of them, speak formally or with an accent?

* Do most, or all of them, always smile?

Try to think of the affluent people you have had a

positive encounter with? Is there a positive character trait that you can identify? Television characters do NOT count! People in the news do NOT count. The people you should be observing here are people you have actually met.

Chapter 3

Truths to embrace

*If you want things to change,
then you have to be willing to do
things you've never done before...*

Along those same lines, you have to be willing to think things you've never thought before. Here are the truths that I embraced and they helped me make significant progress towards my own personal abundance.

* ❖ **The past does not control the future** – The future starts now. Heck, history starts right now. Any past perceived failures or mistakes are now called lessons and they have given you the experience and perspective that you need to move ahead. All life is a teacher and it unfolds perfectly. You needed those lessons to be able to have the perspective you have now. You can bring the lessons/wisdom forward and leave the pain and the experience itself behind.

* ❖ **Where attention goes – energy flows** – You get what you think about. If you're worried about bills, you get more bills. If you're working at

creating income, more income opportunities are created. It truly is as simple as that. It is called the 'Power of Attraction' and it is another reason that 'the rich get richer' and 'the poor get poorer.' The rich think about their money growing and they make glorious fun plans. The poor are worried about making ends meet and visualizing all the bad things that might happen. Visualization can manifest bad things too. Catastrophizing is dangerous conversation.

❖ **If it's available for one, it's available for all –** This Universe does not discriminate – everything is available at all times to everyone. God does not play favorites.

If one person can have a million dollar idea – everyone can. If one person can make a million with their idea – everyone can. It is a matter of where and what we put our attention on.

Go ahead, push back here...

I know I did for many years until I really grasped this concept. Most people will agree that they can have the million dollar ideas – it's the conversion process from idea to reality that is a bit trickier. The problem – at least for me – was once I had the million dollar idea, I started to get tired just thinking about how much work I'd have to do to get it done or how much I'd have to risk to make it work. I'd start to talk myself out of it. I'd start doing calculations and get exhausted by just looking at the numbers. If after trying to talk myself out of it, I still had hope, I knew I could find someone else who could really take the wind out of my sails. I knew how to let myself off the hook!

*Okay, stop pushing back,
let's move forward...*

It is easy to grasp that these ideas are available to everyone. Then remember one more thing – "Ideas are God's gold coin!" So, let's just leave it right there... for now.

* ❖ **One manifester is more powerful than 100 non-manifesters** – Sometimes it seems that certain people can do amazing things by themselves. They are completely commited to what they are doing and it just seems that the Universe aligns to make it happen. Sour-grapes grumbles that "They're just lucky." But the truth was said by Johann Wolfgang von Goethe decades ago – "At the moment of commitment, the Universe conspires to assist you."

The authors of the book, *"Secrets to Creating Passive Income"* (also published by Books To Believe In) tell a story of the time they decided to do a 'full-court press' marketing effort for their book – above and beyond anything they'd ever tried before. They started making their plan of writing articles, speaking engagements, publicity stunts and the like. But the day after they finalized their marketing plan, before they had a chance to do any of the tasks on their list, they started to see their sales increase. Their sales increased 10 fold – overnight – and they hadn't done anything yet.

They set aside their marketing plan for the moment to work on fulfillment of the product and to answer all the fan mail that came in from it – scratching their heads the whole time... what caused the leap in sales?

After about 2 weeks into this wild ride, they received an e-mail that said, "I read about you in Essence magazine and I can't afford your book yet, but I will get it as soon as I get paid. I just want to thank you for writing something that helps other people. Bless you."

Grateful to learn the source of the sales increase, EJ & John wrote back to this woman and of course, sent her a free autographed copy of their book.

The authors had never even considered Essence magazine in their marketing strategy – their strategy was much more grass roots. However, somewhere, somehow, something was put into play – months prior – to have a national magazine mention their book in one of their articles. Someone had to have read the book, whether it was the writer of the article or not. There had to have been some editorial decisions about whether or not it was the best book to choose for the step it was listed under, and so on...

So, explain the timing... the authors were serious about marketing their book, but before they could implement their plan, something 10 times greater than what they had planned happened 'for them'.

At the moment of commitment, the Universe conspires to assist you. ~ Johann Wolfgang von Goethe

**It is just a belief system,
but almost every religion
says they believe it!**

"It is the good pleasure of the Father / God / Universe to give you the Kingdom / abundance / everything."

The religions of the world have golden thread of truths that they all share. One of the great ones of course, is the golden rule, but another very basic one is the theme that God is the provider and he wants us <u>all</u> "to have it all".

❖ *New Testament: Father's good pleasure to give you the kingdom*

❖ *Old Testament: Delight in the Lord, and he will give you the desires of your heart.*

❖ *New Thought: Think and grow rich and the law of attraction*

And there are many other examples...

It is the core belief here that is important and that the Universe/God/etc has the prosperity we all seek and It/He/She will flow in abundance, once we get in proper alignment with it.

However, a shift has to take place, and that shift is up to the individual.

I guarantee, that whatever spirituality you practice, you will find something similar. If I didn't list yours above, find it in your holy writings. When you know which one yours is, print it, frame it and keep it in plain sight, so that you can remember, that in this quest, you have divine help.

Passive Income > Expenses = Financial Freedom

Financial freedom is easy to calculate.

Figure out your budget and find your freedom number – include in it a tithe to a worthwhile cause, taxes, insurance and savings.

Finding your "freedom number" – even if it is a big goal and calling it that instead of calling it "your budget" or "your necessary income" starts to provide a different feeling about what it is you're trying to accomplish. Put it in your journal and then write it on another piece of paper and keep it in front of you...

Passive Income Goal /
Freedom Number:
#######

After you've implemented some of these strategies and the money starts to flow, start recognizing progress (it's more about positive direction of change than about what hasn't happened yet). The progress can be and should be recognized and held in gratitude. As the increases are noticed, say things like, "Wow, now my car is financially free." Or "Now all my utilities are paid for without me having to work for it anymore." Acknowledging and appreciating progress will help you keep and build momentum.

Chapter 4

Insta-cash exists

Lots of sources of
Insta-cash exists.

You need to realize that not only does insta-cash exist, but that it is possible for you to tap into the flow of it.

Insta-cash, or unexpected income, comes to people all over the world, every day, in amazing amounts. Once you start to see the possibilities, you can start to build up a realistic 'How' expectation. Once your 'How' becomes realistic for you, it becomes the solid foundation to the bridge that will take you to your financial freedom.

You could find a big bag of cash on the side of the road

But much more likely is that you'll just find cash everywhere you look. My husband and I find money almost every time we're out and about. Of course, there are hotspots, like underneath the checkstand of a self-checkout kiosk. We find money daily, pennies, dimes, nickels, quarters, and dollar bills everywhere.

For some weird and unexplained reason, we ususally find it 11 cents at a time. That's kind of our number.

Many times, my husband and I will be engaged in a conversation and we will have just made a decision we feel good about and then we'll find some money. At that point, we pick up the money, raise it to the sky and say, "Thanks for the gift and thanks for the endorsement!"

It isn't that we're just lucky to find so much cash, we actually expect to. However, we're not disappointed if we don't find it. We pay close attention to the places where we've found lots of it – like the kiosks, but we literally find it everywhere. We expect it and when we receive it, we show gratitude. It is in my belief system, that those two elements (positive expectation and gratitude) are all we need to have this type of insta-cash perpetually manifest for us.

Your boss could
give you a bonus

In the words of Roger from *Angels in the Outfield* – "It could happen!" Usually you know when your boss has the ability to give you a raise or a bonus, but not always. When you start listening for stories about unexpected bonuses on the job, you'll hear a lot more of them. However, if it isn't even on your radar screen, you probably haven't heard of too many or even hold it out as a possibility in your situation. It may be a probability or it may not be – but it is always a possibility.

You could be asked to do a side job because you are so skilled

If you're well-skilled at something and have done work for others, especially if you've done a good job, you'll get referred for it. Determine for yourself if there is a skill you have that you could do for money and if you're open to receiving work opportunities. Once you start envisioning the possibilities, you either start to work pro-actively to find clients, or they miraculously (it seems) start to look for you.

Do you work with your hands? Can you build or repair something like a deck on the back of a house?

Can you clean well? Does anyone you know need help cleaning that could pay you?

Do you like to cook? Offer to cook and freeze a dozen home made dinners for whatever price you set fit and see if you get any single guys tired of their fast food diet take you up on the deal... Or elderly people who would like a change of pace...

Do you like to read? Can you proof-read someone else's work? Find a writer's group on meetup.com and let them know you're starting work as a book proof-reader. *Hey, if you find any mistakes in this book, I put them there just so you could see if you liked to do this!!!* Millions of web pages also need good proof readers. If you come across a website with a mistake, write to the webmaster, let him know you've already found mistakes on the website and offer to proof read the website for $xxx/webpage. You set your own price. Make it worth your while. If they take your deal – great – if they don't, no worries... There's plenty more where that came from. If they don't pay, they don't get to find out where the error is...

The likelihood that you can make some side money doing something that you like to do and are good at, is high. Take some time and figure out what that is – and be open to the possibilities and let the Universe fill in the blanks.

Find a gift card that
still has money on it

Have you ever lost a gift card that still had money on it? Have you found it yet? Some one else might have. The number of gift cards given out every year is staggering and growing! The number of ones that go uncashed is also growing every year, whether you find one in your wallet from a couple of years ago or you find one on the ground in a parking lot, the odds are good there is money on it. It is finding money!

You could be in the right
place at the right time and
take a photograph that
goes viral on the Internet

Did you see the photo of the "Crasher Squirrel"? Google it – it is adorable. They didn't plan it, it just happened to them. It was a great gift to them from the Universe. Look at the wikipedia page for all the good things that have happened to them since they took that picture. It is astonishing. Crasher Squirrel is now even an iPhone app!

Has there ever been a time when you saw something stunning and you knew, that if you'd have been able to take a photograph, you could have sold it for big bucks? If you're good with a camera, keep one closeby, you just never know when the million dollar picture is right there. At least open up that possibility by having the appropriate tool with you!

Someone from your deep past could pay you a debt they owe you

If someone owes you money, they know it and it weighs on them. If someone owes you money and they come into a great deal of money, they will pay you back. The likelihood that they could read this book is just as high as the likelihood you're reading it. What if they took it to heart, found their financial freedom and in an effort to clear up their sense of self-worth, they send you a check for what they owe you? This happens all the time. In the class I took twice (detailed later), some of the most heartfelt stories were about people who were paid back a debt from long ago and in most cases, long forgiven. The repayment was unexpected and emotional for both parties.

If someone owes you money, send them this book as a present. Who knows...

You could recommend one of your friends to your dentist and the dentist could send you a referral check thanking you.

Many business people pay referral bonuses for people who refer clients to them. For dentists, insurance agents, realtors, financial counselors word of mouth is a tremendously successful marketing tool. Go visit the Chamber of Commerce in your area and get a list of their members. Call and find out if they pay for customer referrals – some most definitely will. Then figure out how you can gracefully refer your friends, family and co-workers to them.

My publisher pays a referral fee for clients referred to her. Know any authors who want their book published? It could be worth money to you.

A rich relative could remember you in his/her will / life insurance

This is the one of the oldest get-rich-quick schemes there is – get a death benefit from someone close to you. It is a harsh way to receive money, but it is one way that money comes to you that you didn't directly earn. Of course, most people's hope is that some distant relative with no other family dies, so you have no emotional loss when they show up at your door with the news. We all do know that this does happen. So this source of unexpected income is very real, however probably painful. Filling out your info at Ancestry.com might enable those distant relatives to find you...

Discover Unclaimed property

There is an amazing system mandated by the government called "Unclaimed Property". This is a holding area for cash that belongs to people who don't know they are entitled to it. One example of unclaimed property is a tax return check that couldn't be forwarded on to the payee. The government doesn't just get that money back – it has to sit in Unclaimed Property Funds giving the payee a chance to claim it for many years. Similarly, all the states and their tax returns that get returned to them have similar funds with similar rules. Other types of unclaimed property include abandoned bank accounts, trust funds and dividend checks due stockholders. Every company in America has rules that govern this type of property, so the types of this kind of property are too vast to go into here.

Every state has a website to help you find out if you have any property to claim. So, for every state you've ever lived in, visit that website and do a query. You won't know unless you go looking, but there are billions of dollars worth of property out there just looking for its rightful owner.

Also, if you were someone's executor or beneficiary, you can search for their names and see if they have something left to be claimed. If you can show your connection through a will or other legal document, there are procedures in place to claim that as well.

If you get good at this, you can query for other family members or friends. If you find something – ask for a finder's fee.

Class action lawsuit

I'd written the above subject line with the intent of researching how many class action lawsuits there were each year in an effort to show you how many people actually get checks like this. At the time I started this book, I had only ever received these letters in the mail that said I could join into a class action because I was a client at some given time. I tended to ignore these unless I do some research because these types of letters could easily end up being some type of phishing scheme. However, just yesterday – during this writing time, I received a check in the mail from an insurance company that said, "The enclosed check is your portion of a class action settlement." It was for $18.70. It is true, these checks do actually just 'appear' in mailboxes all over the US. The only necessary qualification I needed was that I had 2 cars on an insurance policy during a given time frame – which I did.

As if that wasn't enough, two days after this check came in, another offer for a class action lawsuit came in from an old mortgage I held over 5 years prior. I went from having no experience here to 1 check and 2 potential checks. I'm going to write about winning the lottery now...

Check or rebate check in the mail

Every February, I receive a check in the mail FROM the utility company. I never expect it or count on it, but it is a dividend check because I was their customer for several years and apparently, since it was member-owned, there is a residual cash benefit. It is always pleasant when that happens.

Rebate offers are everywhere, some work and some don't. I apply for most of the ones I'm eligible for, however, I don't expect much. When one shows up, whether I've applied for it or not, I celebrate. It is always a nice surprise.

Money could just appear
in your bank account

It doesn't happen very often, but three times over the past 10 years, I've woken up to find an extra $1000 - $2000 in the bank because of back child support. If you have this situation in your life, it could easily happen. If someone does owe you back child support, there is an army of people working to find them and get you paid. It does happen. It happened to me 3 times so far.

"Tip jar" on a website

If you're web-saavy, then you probably know that you can just put a tip jar out on a website and people can donate to it if they feel so led.

You can build a website (there are so many tools now to help the technically challenged). If you decide to 'give away' information, be sure and leave a 'tip jar' on your website. This mechanism allows the person browsing to pay you for your content voluntarily.

Does this really work?

Why would anyone pay if they didn't have to?

It does work. One of my husband's colleagues wrote a technical book that was deemed 'unpublishable' by his publisher just before they were supposed to release it. So this author put the book out on his website – and asked visitors to leave a $12 donation if they liked the content or found it useful. More than 2000 people paid him the $12 donation. You can often count on the fact that the vast majority of the human race is decent, fair and generous and if you give someone something nice, the tendency is that they will give something nice back to you.

Cash in on the 'rewards' on your bank or credit card account.

Does your bank or credit card company offer a 'rewards' program? Do you know how to cash that in for cash? Many of these businesses offer these great programs, but make cashing in on them difficult. However, by applying just a little effort, one can usually cash these rewards in for cash. Many of the businesses that offer these incentives literally bank on the fact that you'll forget. It is money you're entitled to. Go get it.

You could find cash on your doorstep from a caring anonymous friend or relative

Any citizen in the US is allowed to give a gift – tax-free to someone else up to $11,000 – and the recipient doesn't have to a pay a penny in tax. (Be careful, I learned of this when someone was pitching a Ponzi scheme to me, but it is truth – check it out at IRS.gov.)

There are people who quietly gift other people they feel are in need. I have not done this myself, but I do fantasize about the people who I'd help out anonymously when I'm ready to. They are mostly my relatives, who wouldn't take money from me directly... I will do this one day soon.

You could find a piece of a meteorite on the side of the road

Meteorites fall from the sky and have for billions of years. Ordinary people find meteorites frequently, especially if they own any reasonable sized piece of land. Meteorites are owned by the land owner of the land they fall upon. Most people never learn how to distinguish a meteorite from an ordinary rock, (typically magnetic and very heavy), so they see no inherent value in a rock. However, meteorites sell on the open market by the gram – anywhere from an average $5 to $20 per gram depending on the makeup of the meteorrite. There are 28+ grams in an ounce – a single meteorite weighing only an ounce could be worth over $500. Not quite the price of gold, but pretty close.

If you ever find something of value on someone else's land, then strike a deal, create a win/win and get your fair share. A little bit of knowledge always proves to be quite valuable.

Finding something – turning it in and receiving a reward

From lost dogs, lost jewelry to lost wallets, you could come across something that is so dear to someone else that they offer a reward for its return. If you're the fortunate one to find and return it, hundreds to thousands of dollars will be rewarded. If you need to believe that people offer thousands in rewards – check out fidofinder.com.

Keeping your eyes open for things that are out of place is good practice anyway, but there are times when it is a lucrative practice.

Discover a valuable coin in your change

The minting of US silver coins halted in 1964. Most are out of circulation and in the hands of collectors. However, there are still plenty in circulation and occasionally, one shows up in ordinary change. Collectors, when they are looking for more coins, simply buy rolls of coins at the bank and sort through them to see if there are any valuable coins in the mix. Then they wrap the ordinary coins back up and exchange them for new rolls of coins to sort. Silver is trading at an all-time high and articles on the Internet profess that it is possible to make over $1000/month by just sorting coins.

Find something valuable cleaning your attic and post it as an auction item on E-bay

Finding items to sell on E-bay or Amazon.com's used book store is relatively easy for most people, just look in the basement. The old adage, "One man's trash is another man's treasure," has been demonstrated time and time again with E-bay items.

The way to create a bidding war for these items is to take time in the description area and really describe the positive attributes. If you can describe the item in the terms of the buyer – what they'll get out it – instead of just describing the item objectively, you'll have a better chance of creating a desire for it. If you can create the desire for the item with several people, then you'll have a good auction, and with any luck – a bidding war... The secret isn't in the item itself, but in how you describe it. Writing the description to the potential buyer – in the 2nd person (emphasis on 'you'), will give your items an edge over most of the items on E-bay. Take great care with the photography as well and post only terrific pictures of the item.

Don't have an attic - try an estate or garage sale. You might just be able to spot an item you can clean up or fix and then sell on e-Bay, Craigslist or the like.

Whole reality shows are dedicated to this very prospect.

Kindness to a stranger – receive an amazing gift

Many an urban legend has been told about this from Howard Hughes to Mrs. Nat King Cole. However, the fact remains that many people find themselves in need and if someone helps them, they do feel the need to repay. Just being kind to other people gives most people a great feeling and feeling good is a part of this abundance equation. So, even if the gift is just an amazingly good feeling, being kind is its own reward, but who knows...

Service industry – receive an amazing tip

Along those same lines, every now and again, in the service industry, people receive incredibly generous tips. If you work in the service industry, just be open and let the abundance flow in.

Be discovered

Does your dream of prosperity involve fame and fortune? Do you need to be discovered? It is happening everyday. Some on a very grand scale. Susan Boyle comes to mind. 'Golden Voice' as he is known was discovered and his life of being homeless changed instantly into one where he was very much in demand. Both of those are extreme cases, but they absolutely prove the phenomenon of the overnight sensation. It does happen and if it can happen to them, it can happen to you. That's a Universal principle.

Someone could just show up
and give you cash...

This might sound far-fetched, but I took these examples straight out of the news.

❖ Then, as one man described, just as the 31 men were about to leave, an "angel" showed up with an impromptu gift. The man, who preferred to remain anonymous, asked the strangers to line up inside the Labor Finders building. Looking each day laborer in the eye, he handed each a $100 bill.

❖ Woman gives away $100 / day for a year. By Dec. 31, Betty Londergan will have given away $36,500 of her money to charity. For every single day in 2010, Londergan, a Yellow Bluff resident, donated $100 to a cause, person or organization she felt worthy to receive charity in the form of money. As a freelance writer and advertiser, she decided to take the craft she loves the most and expand upon it in what she felt was a unique and giving way. For 365 days, she blogged about why she chose to give to a particular cause and the special people she met along the way.

**Some things you have to activate -
and come with risk, however they
do pay off big occasionally...**

You could win the lottery

You could – it happens everywhere everyday. People are winning the multi-million dollar jackpots, but they are also winning $100, $1000, $10,000 amounts in much greater frequency. If you play the lottery, start to expect to win the larger amounts. In fact, don't purchase a ticket until you're sure that it is possible. If you've ever said to yourself, "I don't win anything." or anything similar, stay completely away from activities where you have to pay to play.

❖ **Win the raffle when you're attending an event**

❖ **You could win a contest**

❖ **You could win the sweepstakes**

- ❖ **You could win McDonald's Monopoly^R**

Tithing on Unexpected income

There is a church in Denver that teachs a course called 'Beyond Limits'. I've taken the course twice. It is a 10-week course. Each time I took it, there were about 200 people or so enrolled. As a way to teach people the power of tithing, the instructor asked the students to tithe on any 'unexpected income' that came to them during the class. If money came in unexpectedly, they were asked to give 10% of it to the church for a specific charity inside the church. Every week, the new total was read and it was astounding how much money was in the fund. By the end of the class, after 8 weeks of giving (first and last class weren't included), we had raised $5000+ in the first class and $7000+ in the second class. That means that over $50,000 of unexpected income came to the members of the first class in two months time and likewise, $70,000 for the second class.

Doing the math, that's $70,000 / 200 people roughly equals $350 / person. That's $175 a month in unexpected income – on the average. Where did all this money come from? People found some. People had a fortuitous meeting with some person, possibly a client, maybe a relative – who knows. Some people were given bonuses and raises at work that they weren't expecting. Some people got checks from people who have owed them money for a long time. Some people won on a lottery ticket. The stories were far more fantastic than most of

us imagined could happen to just normal people like us –
it was really a stunning experience.

As with the power of Attraction, once you are aware
of something, you see it much more often. $175/month
might not be enough to lift you to your Financial
Freedom number, but it is a pretty good personal raise.
It could easily help you to build the foundation on that
bridge to your Financial Freedom.

This was a specific exercise to prove to us that our
jobs were not the only 'source' we could tap into. Our
source is much greater than any job could hold, this type
of source has much more to do with who we are and
aligning up with the prosperous belief systems so that we
help ourselves instead of self-sabotage. Point taken!

**Now, take a moment, take out your journal and
make a list of all the times you received unexpected
income in your life. Use the above examples if you
need a place to start brainstorming, however I'm
certain there are millions of other ways that
unexpected income manifests for everyone.
Recognize yours and take a moment and be grateful
for each and every cent.**

Chapter 5

Proactive Insta-cash (or paychecks by choice)

Think about great things and
great things happen...

Why are there so many Internet millionaires? Why do each of them have a product to sell you about how fast you can get rich on the Internet? Because it is one arena that is ripe for the picking!

If you are resistant to this idea, I must remind you that you can't get out of the problem with the same mind that got you into it, so please be open to this line of thinking – because it is so "rich," in so many ways. Stay with me here, because being very technically proficient is not necessary anymore. Of course it helps, but it is not required.

The Internet is the greatest collaboration tool ever invented. Great websites like Amazon.com have created affiliate programs to help everyone who wants to get a piece of their 85 billion dollar empire to get it. By having so many strategic partners, Amazon.com gets promoted in a far greater way than if they were working by themselves to promote their products. It's a win/win philosophy that helped build them to the super giant corporation that they are.

This philosophy has been emulated all over the Internet. So there are tons of affiliate opportunities to tap into, there are tons of possibilities to cash in on, on someone else's web presence.

Twitter.com /
Amazon Associate combination

Amazon's affiliate sales are one way that anyone that wants to can generate their own paycheck. Combine that with a Twitter.com account and you can Twitter about the deals on Amazon.com. You don't need a web presence or even to know much more than how to press buttons. These two corporations have worked together to create a connection to help co-promote each other – and anyone else that wants to use the connection.

Here's an idea (and it is just one of a thousand possible strategies): Amazon.com changes its sales ranks once an hour. Tweet from Amazon.com once an hour from the page of the #1 book. Use at least one power word (a word in a tweet preceeded with a # sign like #Author), to help people find your tweet and click on your link. This will create a program for you where you are tweeting about something very popular which is what people on Twitter are usually looking for, using a power word will give you an edge and people will click into your Amazon.com affiliate account and if they buy ANYTHING – you get a commission. It's a real way to create a real paycheck.

Share this idea with your family and friends, and get them all to choose a different category (there are hundreds) on Amazon.com – have one do the best 'automotive product' or 'pet product' or 'health product' or 'grocery product' or 'sporting goods', etc, etc, etc...

Amazon.com has millions of products, so there's plenty of opportunity to share this without anyone competing with anyone else.

Squidoo.com

Squidoo.com is a place where any novice can create a webpage with affiliate links that pay commissions. Squidoo.com has partnered with dozens of people that allow affiliate commissions – Amazon, Google, E-bay, etc. They've done all the set up. They want users to create lenses (their name for their webpages) on any topic the user wishes. Then find ways to engage their pre-approved affiliate set with your lens. If you do, they split the affiliate commission with you. If you live in a state where Amazon.com limits you (Colorado, North Carolina and Rhode Island), you can still participate through Squidoo.com.

Put up a blog or a website and put a "tip jar" on it

Did you watch the movie Julie and Julia? This is a real life example of doing just this. Find something to blog about consistently and just talk about it. The woman who gave away the $100/day talked about it on her blog. Her blog was so popular, she made much more than she gave away. Come up with an idea or a concept, then log on to the Internet - grab a blog at Google.com/Blogger or any of the other blog sites and just start journalling your thoughts.

Kindle books

Dust off those old short stories, poems or recipes or write a how-to book about how companies like yours 'should be run.' Teach someone an appreciation for something you love or that you've gone through. In the words of my publisher, "The Day of the Micro-book has dawned!" Kindle books are easy to publish yourself and Amazon.com pays 70% to the self-publisher of those books (if they are priced between $2.99 and $9.99) It truly is easy money...

Make something

If you enjoy making things with your hands, make and sell them on E-bay. Again, be sure the description is all about the benefits for the buyer. With this built-in advertising and distribution system, you can have a full-fledged store and never leave your house! The old issues surrounding distribution don't exist anymore... If you love making things - make them and sell them.

Photograpy or Drawing

There are many microstock photo websites like Istockphoto, Dreamstime, Shutterstock, etc all of which pay commission for photos that are downloaded from their websites. This is a way to create passive income if you have a digital camera and like to take photographs. There is a vast array of photographic subjects on these sites, take a look and see what is there and determine if you could quickly find or take some photographs that would fit into their categories. Taking pictures without people in them will save you some headaches and hassles regarding 'model releases' but after you do your research, you'll figure out how to handle that as well.

If you search the web, you'll see comments all over the board about how easy it is to make money with images, either through these microstock photo sites or from contests. Digital cameras are great tools for creating unbounded income streams.

Freelancing

Do you have a skill that can be hired out on an hourly basis or a project basis? There are websites who work to match up entreprenuers, authors and small business owners with people who can work with them on a freelance basis. You can generally work on these projects in your own time, however, you'll have to meet the deadlines specified to get paid. Elance.com, Ifreelance.com and other websites do this marrying up of freelancers to freelance projects. Check it out – these and others like these available to you – right now!

Organizing Events

If you are good at organizing, start thinking about creating a show or an event. See who else can benefit and get a sponsor for the event, get vendors and participants. All of these people will pay you to play if you create a dynamic enough event. Attend a trade show or two, attend a crafts bazaar or two, attend an athletic or pet expo, attend a cook-off. Someone had to have an idea for each of these events, organized it and gotten the people to come to it. There are professional event organizers, yes, but there are also many, many more amateur event organizers. Check into corporate sponsorships, if you're reaching the same clientele as a corporation would like to, then the corporation will pay to play. That can be really big bucks!!!

Secrets to Creating Passive Income

If you want some great ideas on what there is to write about, blog about or create a platform about, there is a book I've used in the past called *"The Secrets to Creating Passive Income and becoming financially free"* by EJ Thornton and John Clark Craig.

This book *Finding Your Fortune* is not intended to be a how-to book. Its intention is to completely convince you that there is a wealth of money out there that you can just tap into. There are so many other books out there that teach the specifics. The resource guide at the back of this book lists several that I highly recommend.

Chapter 6

Why Things Work

Almost everything that these prosperity
teachers want to teach you is a belief system,
usually their belief system.

They are adamant about their belief system working, because it worked for them. But why are there so many different teachers and belief systems? Because there are so many different things to believe in. So, in that sense, all of these prosperity tools work and they work well for those that believe in the system.

If you've ever tried some of these and they didn't work for you, it is because you didn't buy into the belief system deeply enough to make a real shift in your circumstances. Yes, it goes back to you — not them. Everything in life that affects you does ultimately go back to you — no one else. You have to take responsibility for your own life and circumstances if you ever want to change it, especially if you want to change it dramatically.

So, below, I will talk about some of the prosperity theories I've had personal experience with and tell you what I think their secret is and why if you used it and it didn't work for you, what might have been the 'disconnect.' This is, of course, all just my opinion, so I want you to apply your own logical thought process and see if you can find a way to make it work for you and try again - if you feel so led.

Getting Happy

This is about changing your attitude towards better feeling and better feeling emotions. The clearest teachers of this are Jerry and Esther Hicks. They actually have a scale of that ranks 22 emotions from the worst feeling to the best feeling emotions. They ask you to figure out where you are and to reach for the next higher emotion until you make it significantly up the scale from where you are.

This has to do with personal responsibility and personal awareness, but what does it have to do with prosperity? Everything, if you listen to their teachings. I recommend their teachings whole-heartedly.

Consistently working to maintain a positive attitude, positive outlook, positive experience and positive expectation are keys to being able to silence the dream-stealers, (especially those in your own head) and reprogram the way you talk about your life and your circumstances.

Being happy (or happier) is reward in itself and once you start to feel the improved circumstances in your psyche, you'll start to have an increasing awareness and appreciation of the good things around you. Once you have an awareness of the good things around you, very likely your level of gratitude will increase and the laws of attraction will start to serve more and more good to you.

If this didn't work for you... likely you were keeping score about how much was or wasn't changing in your immediate circumstances. It is easy to want instant results - especially when the teachers/gurus explain that instant results are possible - once the 'true shift' is accomplished. If your needs are dire, it is hard to find a 'happy place' for long. Ignoring present circumstances isn't generally understood by nagging spouses and hungry children.

However, finding a time and place to truly shut out all the noise and start to work on the way you feel about your future is critical. It it's hard for you 'get away from it all' take advantage of your private time to listen to CD's or breathe deeply or meditate... Take a few more minutes in the shower... Wake up 10 minutes earlier and employ some of that time to connect with yourself and your manifestation power.

I took the mediation CD's of these teachers, downloaded a free sound editing program off the Internet, and recorded a 'white noise' track over it, then made a CD of the combined tracks. My idea was that my subconscious still hears through the white noise. I put this recording in a CD player repeating the track all through the night. This way I could listen all night to teachings and let them seep into my subconscious enabling the teachings "in" farther. It was relaxing to drift off to sleep to the white noise, especially with the added thought that the white noise was really going to be good for me.

You have to stop keeping score about what hasn't happened yet, and get very much in tune with the things in your life that are working, that you are grateful for. You have to completely turn your attention away from what's missing to blessing what's already present.

Which brings us to gratitude...

Oprah's Gratitude Journal

On January 1, 2008, Oprah suggested that we all start creating "Gratitude Journals". She instructed that we all get a journal and write in it for 5 minutes a day all the things we were grateful for. Much like Jerry and Esther's "Book of Positive Aspects", the gratitude journal was to contain only positive thoughts. She interviewed guest after guest who told the story about this exercise changing their lives. Go ahead and google, "Oprah's Gratitude Journal" and read the testimonials.

Committing time on a daily basis to write about positive things does several great things, such as create an increased awareness and appreciation of the good things around you. Even if it is difficult at first to find the good things, they do exist. Looking for them turns your focus away from problems and on to blessings - and that is good for you as well.

Shifting thoughts toward gratitude is powerful for so many objectives and creating prosperity is, of course, one of the big ones. Just like 'getting happy,' the law of attraction is on your side with this exercise and once you start finding things to be grateful for, the Universe will start to serve up more and more things for you to be grateful for. It is the law...

If this didn't work for you, again, my guess is that you were keeping score. Any type of measuring on a day to day basis keeps you anchored to circumstances and you need to break free of that long enough to learn to trust that you are supported in this lifetime by these universal truths.

Sitting up straight

I personally love this one, because it so clearly demonstrates the power of a belief system. As described earlier, a fire-walking gentleman observed rich people and saw something he could emulate. When he emulated it, by sitting and standing tall. He was conscious about what he was working toward and he was connecting with his inner-millionaire...

There's a belief system taught by many an MLM called "Fake it 'til you make it.' This 'sitting up straight' works to support that. He acted like 'it'   until he was 'it'.

Fake it 'til you make it...

The advice from many abundance teachers is to go to places where rich people 'hang out' - fancy car dealerships, million-dollar plus houses. The idea here is to get the feel of being rich. Take it in, absorb it into your psyche... Imagine driving the car, sit in the driver's seat if they'll let you, take a test drive if it is possible. The whole time mentally logging what it feels like so that you have a tangible memory of the experience.

When walking through a million-dollar home, you need to put yourself in it - literally and figuratively. Imagine your next Thanksgiving will be in that home. Imagine how many people you'll have over. Imagine where the table will go and what it will look like. Imagine yourself at the head of the table and graciously welcoming all your friends and family to your new home. Smell the food in your mind. Imagine the expressions on the faces around the table as everyone raises their glasses to make a toast to your success and generosity.

If this didn't work for you... then likely, like me, your inner critic came out and constantly reminded you that your were 'faking' it.

Find a way to have your inner-millionaire buy off your inner-critic and send them to the Bahamas for a permanent vacation...

Truly, the answer is to do those types of visualization, getting better and better at them all the time. Make the process a game in your mind and you'll find great enjoyment in the process and in the results. If you can get someone to do it with you – it becomes really fun.

Set the stage... start with the premise that every single plan you have works out perfectly and imagine what that will feel like in a week, a month, a year – five years. Then play the role of yourself, 5 years from now.

Vision boards -
Visioning - Visualization

Many abundance teachers ask their students to create vision boards, do visioning work or visualize their abundance. These are all great - again to connect to the feeling of prosperity. If it is difficult for you to do this, there are so many starter exercises from so many teachers - just open up any book on prosperity training and find one.

My favorite is to imagine and actually create a check register where there is $1000 deposited, and I have to spend the full amount of $1000 that day. I actually have to write out, at least in the check register, what checks I would write and for what. The next day $2000 is deposited and the same rules apply. The next day $3000, $4000 etc. Doing that for a solid month helps connect you to an abundance mind-set, because not only do you have to figure out how to spend the money, the actual act of writing it down and calculating the balances etc... makes it feel more real.

If this didn't work for you, I'd guess that your inner critic was working on you about your 'worthiness' for having great and beautiful things or you were otherwise guilt-tripping about starving children overseas while you were imagining living in the lap of luxury. If you felt any resistance at all, listen to your inner critic to determine the objection, then go talk with your inner millionaire and solve your problem.

Using the same logic, you can't get sick enough to make anyone else well, you can't be poor enough to make anyone else rich (or even less-poor). What you can be is rich enough to become philanthropic and then you can help those starving children much more realistically and practically. While you are writing those checks out, be sure to include some philanthropic giving and imagine how good it feels to truly make a difference in someone else's life by being generous.

Writing out future
paychecks to yourself

As long as we're writing checks...

There are great stories told by several celebrities who wrote checks to themselves and carried them in their wallets or posted them on their bathroom mirrors. They wrote the check they knew that they would someday cash - for an enormous amount of money.

There is a story of a lady who in the 1980's won "Star Search" for acting. Even before she entered the contest, she wrote a check for the full $100,000 prize and posted it on her bathroom mirror. When friends or family questioned her, she would reply, "I know I'm going to get it." And their response, whether supportive or derogatory didn't affect her one way or the other. She held true to her knowing and she indeed did win first place and she cashed a check for $100,000.

Jim Carrey has a similar story. Many other celebrities and millionaires also do.

If this didn't work for you... your inner critic's or outer dream stealer's opinion of what you were doing was more real to you than the receipt of the amount of money on the check. It is easy to let other people's opinions in - and where most people 'mean well' - and don't want you to get hurt by your own high hopes – those well-meaning people actually can do real damage...

The best way to divert a dream stealer - is to give them something else to chew on...

Enter Uncle George...

Uncle George

One of my great uncles was an amazing character - claiming to actually be the first 'streaker' in history, and many more amazing things... however he had some advice for his descendants that belongs in a *'Book of Great Wisdom'*.

Uncle George was born in 1900. He was a school teacher in a small town in Ohio and he chewed tobacco. Not only did he chew it, he was more than a bit obnoxious about it. And the parents of his students complained about it - loudly. But it didn't phase him, he just happily chewed his tobacco.

When one person in a desperate need to understand his behavior finally asked him, "Why don't you just quit chewing tobacco? If you do, they'll stop complaining."

Uncle George replied, "No, they'll never stop complaining, they'll start complaining about something else - and that something else might be a little closer to my heart - like my teaching or my moral fiber. If I give them something obvious to complain about - they'll stay stuck on that and leave the things that really matter to me alone."

So, if you have dream stealers in your life - and you freely share with them what you are doing - with regards to increasing your own personal abundance - and those people insult it - or you... **STOP TALKING ABOUT IT TO THEM!!!** It is likely that they are very bored or discontented in their own lives - and misery loves company - so they tend to be negative about everything in their lives - and in yours...

If you know this is the case, then you need to create a diversion. Create a cause for conversation that they can grab ahold of and run with - that isn't about your self-improvement goals. Do something dramatic...

❖ Dye your hair

❖ Paint a wall in your house some very loud color (like green for abundance)

❖ Take up a new hobby like gourmet cooking, bird watching or astronomy or something else where you can create a lot of conversation

❖ Collect something interesting

Just do something else - interesting. It will create a new focus of attention and end everyone sitting around complaining about their general state of malaise.

Surrounding yourself with symbols of prosperity

Cultures around the world have their own versions of prosperity symbols and symbolism. Prosperity superstitions abound.

Some common symbols include:

- **Painting your door red**
- **Bamboo**
- **Frogs**
- **Chinese Calligraphy**

If these symbols remind you of your prosperity and get you in touch with your inner millionaire, then by all means - surround yourself with them. But more than that, do what the fire-walking gentleman did, and observe life. Figure out what abundance looks like and bring it into you. Is it the things you put on your vision board? Is it something else - only you know. When you find what symbolizes wealth and connects you to it, find a way to surround yourself with it.

Don't be afraid of "I told you so..."

Along the same lines of creating a diversion... if you aren't overt about what you are really working on, you won't let in those immortal and painful words - "I told you so..." when someone else decides to keep score about your progress in life.

If you don't let them in, it won't be an issue. If you've already let them in and they await your results as eagerly as you do - then there are two of you keeping score and anchoring you to circumstances. This gets in the way of creating abundance, if you feel you have to answer to someone else...

If you have already let them into the inner-circle, then stop giving them the updates and change the subject on them... They'll likely forget, but if they don't, just openly ask them to forget about it or set a boundary about it that you aren't willing to talk about it anymore. Eventually, they'll let it go. If they don't, then let them say to you, "I told you so..." all the while knowing they don't have the facts, nor the power to influence you on this path any longer.

No one has to know what you're doing. In fact, most rich people keep their finances and their financial strategies to themselves. Many people consider it entertaining to tell their friends everything they are doing. However, shooting holes in your abundance work should not be considered 'sport' by people who supposedly care about you. Play it close to the vest. And when it works – **laugh to yourself... all the way to the bank.**

Just like with the children on the plane during a disaster, put your own oxygen mask on, then once you're okay financially, then you can teach others how to do it - if you so choose.

As as Plato said...

**You teach best what you
most need to learn...**

You'll actually notice for some of these abundance authors, that they weren't millionaires when they first started to write about becoming millionaires... But they were on a successful path that they truly believed would take them there.

So, they wrote about it. They did this for many reasons. Primarily, writing books or articles is a way to create passive income streams... and their unwavering faith that they had found 'the way to riches' gave them the confidence to write the book even before they reached their abundance goals.

It's a funny thing about abundance goals - they are always changing. Usually when a person reaches one goal, they set a greater one. So, I would bet that the gurus who wrote the books are richer for having written them, and that they still haven't completely reached their abundance goals yet. However, their current abundance goals are much greater than they were when they were writing their book. I would also wager that their initial financial goals were achieved while they were still writing the books.

Why? Because when you teach, you absolutely connect with the truth that you are teaching. You know at a core level that it is real, useful and worth sharing. That core-level shift is what it truly takes to have the instant manifestations the masters speak of.

If you try this, write first before you talk about it to anyone else. Get in touch with your basic belief system and describe fully the pieces of these abundance teachings that you feel are truth and ignore the ones that you don't connect with.

When it all comes down to it, there is a golden thread that runs through all these teachings and if you really study it, you'll figure it out. Once you do, you too will create the core-level shift you need, and your life will never be the same.

Read Napolean Hill's story about how his book "Think and Grow Rich" came about. He was commissioned by Andrew Carnegie to find out what made rich people rich and to write a book on it. Not only did he write the book that is a consistent best-seller even though it was first published in 1937, Napolean Hill also became very rich by studying the habits of rich people.

Several compilation books and movies follow this pattern. They'll find experts in a field and interview them and extract from these experts the core content for the film or book. Rhonda Byrne's The Secret was one such movie – and if you've been paying any attention at all to the abundance channels and Youtube or Facebook, you know how successful that was. Born out of desperation, Rhonda found a pathway to prosperity – and did an amazing job of sharing it with anyone who would listen. By the way, the book that inspired her to begin this quest was called, "The Science of Getting Rich" by Wallace Waddles and it was published in 1910. There's nothing new about abundance and prosperity principles. These are ancient principles.

Faith & perseverance:
"I never stopped believing..."

I've listened to many famous authors, entrepreneurs, millionaires and spiritual masters and I've noticed one true common theme to all their stories. That common theme is perseverance and an unshakable belief in their objective. There are many common threads to their belief systems, but the one common thread to the stories is that they never gave up and always believed in themselves and their ability to accomplish what they set out to do.

Never give up – Never say die – Hold on to your dream – Never let anyone tell you you can't do it... etc.

I used to think that perseverance sounded like a lifetime of struggle – and while I believed that, it was. However, I've come to realize that

"Perseverance is merely going confidently in the direction of your dream – forever!"
**Do What You Love
and the Money Will Follow...**

These are some of the most true words ever spoken. Because once you are doing something you love, you're a happier person. Once you're a happier person, finding things that you can be grateful for is easier. When you are doing something you love, you'll never quit, and you'll believe in it and yourself. When you believe in yourself - you'll be able to make the core-level shift you need to create the abundance in your life.

It sounds trite - but many great truths are very, very simple. This is a great truth.

Chapter 7

It is all about believing

Enjoy & do what you love and the money WILL follow

I hope that this book has given you something to believe in - something real - something believable, possible, tangible, attainable and substantial.

If you'll do the exercises and revisit the programs you've been frustrated with in the past, I hope you'll be able figure out how to get in touch with that inner millionaire of yours and send that inner critic out of the country for good.

There is great truth in almost everyone's abundance systems and you'll find one that connects with you without disrupting any other spiritual belief system you have going. When you do find the one you connect with - go ahead, approach it with a healthy amount of skepticism, because no one path or belief system works for everyone.

If you stick with it, you'll find your rythym, you'll find the sweet spot and you'll prosper - in every sense.

Good luck and please, write to me about how this information was received and perceived by you.

Recommended Reading

All books available on
ForTheWealthOfAll.com

Think and Grow Rich – Napoleon Hill   ISBN: 1936594412

The Secret - Rhonda Byrne   ISBN: 1582701709

The Science of Getting Rich – Wallace Waddles
ISBN: 0984064621

Secrets of the Millionaire Mind – T. Harv Eker
ISBN: 0060763280

Ask and It is Given – Esther & Jerry Hicks ISBN: 1401907997

Spiritual Engineering – Thomas Strawser ISBN: 0984483896

Secrets to Creating Passive Income – EJ Thornton &
John Clark Craig   ISBN: 0980194199

Cash in a Flash – Mark Victor Hanson   ISBN: 0307453316

Rethinking Retirement – Keith Weber   ISBN: 0984541721

Finding Your Soul Mate – Sparkle Phillips
ISBN: 0977996034

The Law of Attraction Made Simple – Jonathan Manske
ISBN: 0980194180

A Great Life Doesn't Happen by Accident – Jonathan
Manske   ISBN: 0984634231

Resources

Beyond Limits Course
http://MileHiChurch.com/courses/beyond_limits.a
sp
This is a 10 week course, taught twice a year.

Go to the website or call them
and they will help you find
a similar course in your area.

About the Author

Sparkle Phillips

Pardon my Anonymity

I'm not going to use my real name – because if I did, I am well enough known – likely, you would know who I am. Since my first book was about relationships and I was brutally honest about some of the men in my life, I kept anonymous to spare their identities. I have to keep honoring that pact.

In the same way that I could talk freely about men in my last book, I can talk freely about mistakes I've made with money, and my thinking around money and anonymity will give me the freedom to tell my story completely and openly without fear of someone else's feelings. If I had to worry about someone else's feelings, I might be tempted to sugar coat or water down an interpretation.

That being said, my toughest criticism will be on myself. I strive to live a completely empowered life and will never claim victim status. I am who I am because of the experiences that brought me thus far on my path.

To paraphrase Richard Bach (one of my favorite authors) – "You gave your life to become who you are today, was it worth it?" My answer is yes. I hope yours is too.

About the Cover

Cover design was done by DesignsByCapri.com.

The use of the yin yang symbol using dollar signs instead of dots is intended to signify two parts who make a complete whole.

The color chosen of course was green to symbolize prosperity. The overall symbolism was intended to match that of the *Finding Your Soul Mate*.

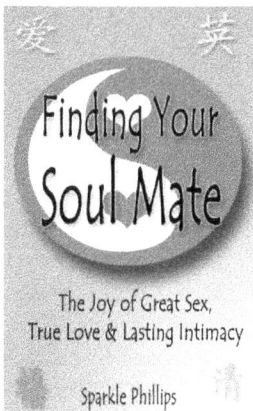

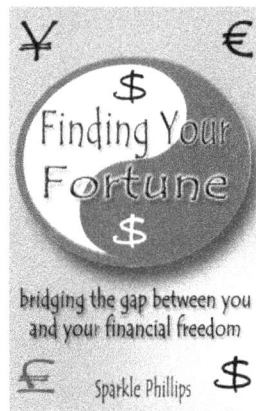

ORDER FORM
Finding
Your
Fortune
$12.97 + 3.50 (S&H)

online at:
http://ForTheWealthOfAll.com

by phone:
have your credit card handy and call:
(303) 794-8888

by fax:
(720) 863-2013

by mail:
send check payable to:
Thornton Publishing, Inc.
17011 Lincoln Ave. #408
Parker, Colorado 80134

Name: _____

Address _____

_____

Phone: _____

E-mail: _____

Credit Card #: _____

Card Type: _____   Expiration Date: ____/____

Security Code: _____

www.ingramcontent.com/pod-product-compliance
Lightning Source LLC
Chambersburg PA
CBHW071625040426
42452CB00009B/1488